THE SOUTH AFRICAN STORY with Archbishop Desmond Tutu

Roger Friedman and Benny Gool

PENGUIN BOOKS

PENGUIN BOOKS

Published by the Penguin Group
Penguin Books (South Africa) (Pty) Ltd, 24 Sturdee Avenue, Rosebank, Johannesburg 2196, South Africa
Penguin Group (USA) Inc, 375 Hudson Street, New York, New York 10014, USA
Penguin Group (Canada), 90 Eglinton Avenue East, Suite 700, Toronto, Ontario, Canada M4P 2Y3 (a division of Pearson Penguin Canada Inc)
Penguin Books Ltd, 80 Strand, London WC2R 0RL, England
Penguin Ireland, 25 St Stephen's Green, Dublin 2, Ireland (a division of Penguin Books Ltd)
Penguin Group (Australia), 250 Camberwell Road, Camberwell, Victoria 3124, Australia (a division of Pearson Australia Group Pty Ltd)
Penguin Books India Pvt Ltd, 11 Community Centre, Panchsheel Park, New Delhi – 110 017, India
Penguin Group (NZ), 67 Apollo Drive, Rosedale, Auckland 0632, New Zealand (a division of Pearson New Zealand Ltd)

Penguin Books (South Africa) (Pty) Ltd, Registered Offices:
24 Sturdee Avenue, Rosebank, Johannesburg 2196, South Africa

www.penguinbooks.co.za

First published by Penguin Books (South Africa) (Pty) Ltd 2011

ISBN 978-0-14-352814-2

Printed and bound by 1010 Printing International Ltd, China

CONTENTS

I come from a beautiful land, richly endowed with wonderful natural resources, wide expanses, rolling mountains, singing birds, bright shining stars, clear blue skies, with radiant sunshine, golden sunshine. There are enough good things that come out of God's bounty, there are enough for everyone.

Let me show you around.

WESTERN CAPE

Cape of Storms

The Cape of Storms, this Gateway to Africa. Sir Francis Drake, on his sixteenth-century voyage around the world, called it 'a most stately thing, and the fairest Cape we saw in the whole circumference of the earth'.

The Cape of Good Hope is so majestic – God did something special here! You really can understand how, when He had created everything, God said, 'Even if I have to say so, this is pretty good work. Looking at the southernmost point of this African continent, I think I've got to do something special here.' This is a place where two oceans meet, and so God put together the mountains and the plants and produced this fantastic gateway in the south.

It was here on these shores, on the slopes of Table Mountain, that more than three centuries ago the fateful convergence of the peoples of Africa, Europe and Asia began.

The South African Story with Archbishop Desmond Tutu

Archaeological evidence of stone-age fish traps, rock art and pottery shards dating back almost two thousand years tell us that the Khoikhoi were probably the first people in the Cape. They called themselves the 'real people'. They were the first inhabitants the Dutch settlers encountered when Jan van Riebeeck and the Dutch East India Company arrived here in 1652 to create a halfway station between Europe and the Far East so that ships rounding the Cape could take on fresh water and other supplies.

You can feel the echoes of our history in the city streets – from the Castle of Good Hope, the original fortress with its green dungeons, to the Victorian buildings that line flamboyant Long Street. The contribution that thousands of slaves made to the development of the Cape is commemorated at the Slave Lodge, which is today a cultural history museum. Three hundred years ago freed slaves congregated on the cobblestones of Greenmarket Square to sell their produce. Today, traders from all over Africa showcase their crafts and curios in this delightful square which is surrounded by cafés and restaurants.

The Bo-Kaap, one of the most colourful districts of Cape Town, is traditionally home to the Cape Malay people, descendants of the political exiles, slaves and convicts the Dutch East India Company brought to Cape Town from Indonesia and India. In 1794, exiled Islamic leader, Tuan Guru, helped establish the city's first mosque in this area.

On the east side of Cape Town is the empty scar of land that once marked the vibrant community of District Six. When the Group Areas Act was introduced, the government tore down the houses and forcibly removed the families who lived here to the barren dustlands of the Cape Flats. Some traumas are not easily resolved, not even years later.

Cape Town today is a city of style, substance and beauty. Its history, architecture, food, and fashion have been influenced by the blood of many nations. It is the home of South Africa's parliament, and our cultural and tourism capital. The Victoria and Alfred Waterfront has been at the heart of the city's development over the past twenty years and is a shopping Mecca, the location of fine hotels and the gateway to Robben Island.

I've been looking at Robben Island from the top of Table Mountain. What exquisite torture it must have been for those who, like Nelson Mandela, spent twenty years or more in the prison there, looking across the ocean and seeing a little freedom. It must have been . . . it must have been hell. The city of Cape Town – so near, yet so far, across an impassable body of water.

Many struggle activists were imprisoned on Robben Island. The prison is now a World Heritage Site and many of the tour guides are former inmates and guards who are willing to forget the past but not let us forget what it meant.

The Winelands is an area just inland from Cape Town and includes the historic towns of Stellenbosch, Wellington and Paarl. The area produces world-class wines in world-class geographic settings, including Pinotage, our own signature variety.

Nelson Mandela, or Madiba as he is so warmly known through his clan name, spent most of the twenty-seven years of his incarceration on Robben Island, but he came here to the Winelands for the last few of those years. And it was here, outside the Victor Verster Prison in the Winelands, that history was made on 11 February 1990. The place was full of jostling humanity, especially journalists and television cameras. It was a beautiful sunny day and people were eager and expectant, waiting for the great moment when Nelson Mandela would walk out of the prison gates. His release was the result of pressure from our incredible friends overseas in the anti-apartheid movement as well as pressure from within our country. And it was as though our Berlin Wall had fallen.

We have a lovely African word which is very difficult to put into other languages: *Ubuntu*, *Botho*. It speaks about our interconnectedness. *I am, because you are*. And we say, *a person is a person through other persons*. We are interconnected, all of us.

FREE STATE

Riding the Plains

If you wish to experience the expansiveness of our beautiful South Africa, then this is the place to which to come. Nelson Mandela said of this province: 'No matter what my mood, when I am here I feel that nothing can shut me in, that my thoughts can roam as far as the horizon.'

Deep beneath the fertile earth are vast subterranean fields of the precious metal for which South Africa is renowned. Everything in the Free State seems orangey-gold, the maize fields, the acres of sunflowers, the way the setting sun strikes the sandstone cliffs of the Golden Gate, surely one of our most beautiful national parks.

It was here that King Moshoeshoe had to balance the interests of his Basotho people against expansionist English trade and Dutch farming interests, making decisions that ultimately led to the creation of the British Protectorate of Basutoland, now the Kingdom of Lesotho. I served as the bishop of Lesotho for some years and the country has a very special place in my heart. It's a rugged mountain country, but the Basotho people are so warm, so hospitable – and as tough as the environment in which they live.

The distinctive blankets you'll see the Basotho people wearing, and I have one on my shoulder, date back to a gift presented to King Moshoeshoe by a European trader in 1860. And, you know how it is with fashion, within a few years everyone was wearing them. The designs on the blankets are an important part of family life, signifying major events from marriage to manhood to the birth of your first child.

They are a good example of how we in Southern Africa absorb things from different cultures and make them uniquely our own. These blankets may feature designs of mealies, a symbol of fertility, or the crocodile, an animal sacred to the Basotho, but you'll also find blankets sporting images of imperial crowns or even British warplanes!

The Free State's gold fields produce a third of the country's gold, but this province is also South Africa's bread basket producing 70 per cent of the country's maize – our staple food. It is the bountiful and nourishing pantry of South Africa.

An important struggle landmark in the town of Brandfort is the house where Winnie Madikizela-Mandela was once exiled.

I visited her several times during her exile, to bring her Holy Communion – to remind her that she could never be exiled from God and the wider community of faith. Of course the time in Brandfort took its toll on her, but it could not defeat her spirit.

House arrest was one of the apartheid government's most insidious punishments for activists they perceived to be troublemakers. Winnie was cut off from friends and family in a remote place where she couldn't speak the language; she was under house arrest for nine years in a shack with no floors or ceiling, no running water or electricity. She was an exile in her own country. Security police were later to apply for amnesty to the Truth and Reconciliation Commission for twice setting fire to her home.

Bloemfontein, the capital, is known as the city of roses and is the judicial seat of the country. The Supreme Court of Appeal here has seen landmark appeal cases, redefining the definition of marriage, for example, to pave the way for gay marriage to become legal. Justice has prevailed through the courageous fight for its survival by people of all races in this country.

About seventy years before Winnie was put under house arrest in Brandfort other forms of detention were being applied with vigour in the Free State – in the British concentration camps of the second Anglo-Boer War. Really, it should be called the South African War, because it wasn't only between the British and the Boers. Many black South Africans were drawn into the war on both sides. And, although the British ultimately defeated the Boers, after the peace treaties were signed the biggest losers were black South Africans.

It was a ruinous, terrible war. The Boers relied on guerrilla warfare, making lightning strikes against the regimented British forces before retreating to the hills. To try to cut the Boers off from their support network and supplies, Lord Kitchener authorised two tactics that would take a terrible toll – a scorched earth policy of burning farms, and concentration camps.

AFSKEID · 11-10-1899

The South African Story with Archbishop Desmond Tutu

The conditions in these camps were shocking – so shocking that by the end of the war, more women and children had died than combatants. In a Brandfort children's camp, 375 children died in one month alone. By the end of the war, the death toll stood at 27 000 Boer women and children and 20 000 black South Africans.

At that time there was another woman in the Free State who spoke out fearlessly against her government and the terrible things they were doing. Her name was Emily Hobhouse and she became known as the turncoat heroine for her campaign in Britain against the shocking conditions in the camps where rations were in short supply and overcrowding and disease were rife.

It's a difficult thing to be a lone voice standing up to authority. People associate courage with lions and dragons, but real courage is being a mouse surrounded by lions and dragons and yet still speaking out.

There's a saying that the Free State is so flat that you can see right into tomorrow. How far could King Moshoeshoe see, could Emily Hobhouse see, could Winnie Mandela see? One can but marvel at the Free State's evolution. From free land of the San through the times of the Sotho-speaking kings; from British Sovereignty to Independent Boer Republic to province of the apartheid Republic; from scorched earth to the breadbasket of our new democracy. From a 'free' republic for some to a free country for all.

NORTH WEST

Platinum Province

The area known as the Cradle of Humankind is a World Heritage Site which straddles the Gauteng and North West provinces, covering 474 square kilometres. The fossils cradled within its rocks provide evidence of the evolution of human beings – you and me!

This is where it all started. The iron in this dusty red earth runs in the blood of all our veins. The sunny weather warmed our bones and helped us to make that giant leap from *Homo habilis* to *Homo sapiens*. It doesn't matter what we look like, or even where we come from – millions of years ago, we all took our first steps here. So, we are *all* African!

The Cradle of Humankind encompasses thirteen key sites including the famous Swartkrans, where we find evidence of the first controlled use of fire a million years ago. Our early ancestors took burning coals, probably from fires caused by lightning, and managed to keep them burning. We South Africans love our braais. Well, perhaps the first one happened right here in the Cradle of Humankind!

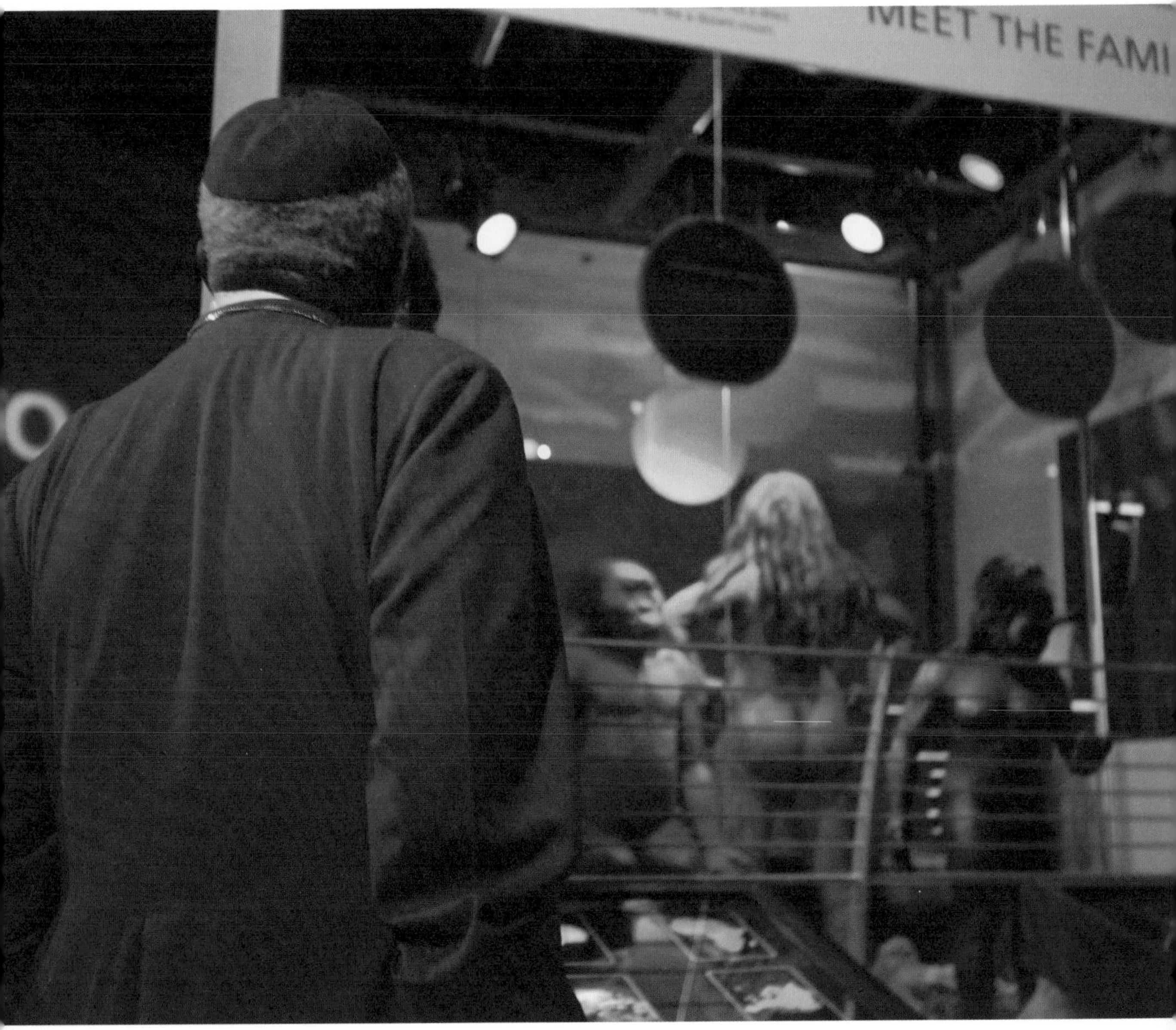
MEET THE FAMI

'Maropeng' is a Setswana word which means 'returning to the place of origin' and it is the official visitor centre in The Cradle. A massive burial mound called the Tumulus is the entrance to a world-class interactive exhibition focusing on the development of humans over the past few million years. From a scientific point of view it tells us about our history – where we came from, where we grew up, even what we looked like. And it is something to be immensely proud of.

In 1947 Robert Broom, a South African doctor and palaeontologist, found an adult female skull in the Sterkfontein caves close to Maropeng. It was dubbed 'Mrs Ples' – short for *Plesianthropus transvaalensis*. Here at Sterkfontein the world's longest sustained fossil excavation began in 1966 and it continues to the present day. More than five hundred hominid specimens have been unearthed, making it the world's richest hominid site.

Today, the Bafokeng, or 'People of the Dew', own about 70 000 hectares of land in the North West province. History tells us that as people moved around from place to place, they came here and saw that the grass was heavy with dew. They realised that this was somewhere with plenty of water where they could live and their animals could graze. But it turned out that there was not just dew on the grass – there was something underneath!

The astute Chief Mokgatle sent young Bafokeng men to Kimberley to work on the diamond mines, and when they came home their earnings went into a kitty that helped buy the land that today belongs to the Bafokeng people. Their diligence was rewarded with the discovery of chrome and platinum on the mineral rich Merensky Reef.

The Merensky Reef has the world's second largest deposit of platinum. In the beginning the Bafokeng were paid a pittance by mining companies for the wealth extracted from their land. But eventually they prevailed. Their policy of charging mining giants to mine the land has paid off handsomely and they have been able to develop schools, roads and clinics.

This house was the King's home in the 1930s and 40s and it is now an important Bafokeng heritage site. The area is known as Direpotsane (a hill) and from here you can see many of the twenty-nine Bafokeng villages.

The totem of the Bafokeng tribe is the crocodile. The Bafokeng Queen Mother, Semane Molotlegi, tells us that the Bafokeng crocodile has a closed mouth which symbolises the fact that the Bafokeng don't speak a lot. Instead, they act!

Less uplifting stories of social engineering in South Africa are those of the apartheid homelands. Here in the North West a 'separate country' called Bophuthatswana was mapped out for the Tswana-speaking black people.

The so-called president of Bophuthatswana, Lucas Mangope, was not keen to relinquish power and have his country reincorporated into South Africa prior to the first democratic elections in April 1994. But shortly before the elections Mangope's defence force mutinied, he was unseated and the land was reintegrated into South Africa.

Mmabatho, formerly the capital of Bophuthatswana, is today the capital city of North West province.

If you are into more flamboyant architecture than that of Mmabatho, you may wish to try The Palace of the Lost City for size. The royal towers rise above the dense surrounding bush, drawing thousands of visitors every year into its walls and entertainment halls. The Palace of the Lost City is one of four hotels within the Sun City casino and luxury holiday resort, opened by hotel magnate Sol Kerzner in 1979 in what was then still Bophuthatswana. In those days all forms of gambling, apart from horse racing, were illegal in South Africa.

The South African Story with Archbishop Desmond Tutu

Next door to Sun City is the Pilanesberg Game Reserve, home to the full menu of animals of the South African plains. The Pilanesberg used to be home to BaTswana people, but in 1979 Operation Genesis displaced the BaTswana to make way for the largest game resettlement project in the history of South Africa. Six thousand animals from other parks were settled here and it is a popular destination for locals and tourists alike.

Another spot especially popular with visitors from Johannesburg and Pretoria is the Magaliesberg, where people come to escape the city over the weekend. This mountain range stretches for over 120 kilometres from Bronkhorstspruit Dam east of Pretoria all the way to Rustenburg.

The Magaliesberg are among the oldest mountains in the world, dating back some two billion years, more than a hundred times older than Mount Everest. There are wonderful ravines – some 100 metres deep – with crystal clear streams, waterfalls and sheer quartzite cliffs.

At the foot of the Magaliesberg lies the mining town of Rustenburg. The name, translated from Dutch, means 'Place of Rest'. Rustenburg is the platinum hub of South Africa and the two largest platinum mines in the world are found here – Amplats and Impala Platinum Holdings. The area also produces asbestos, tin, chrome, lead, marble, granite and slate.

Our people are amazing in so many ways. Yet fifteen years down the line after democracy, the so-called 'freedom dividend' is something not all have yet experienced. You know, we do have a fantastic country, a beautiful country with wonderful people. But we really ought to be making it an even more caring community.

We have enough resources in our country for everyone to be able to live comfortably. All of our children should be able to go to the schools they want to go to, every single person here should be able to have a decent home. I hope we can do that.

MPUMALANGA

Land of the Rising Sun

Mpumalanga, the 'land of the rising sun' as it is known to its Siswati and Zulu-speaking residents, is a place of forests and waterfalls, deep canyons, thorny bushveld and the Big Five. It is a place of awe-inspiring vistas and daily dramas, a window into the cycle of life.

Let's start at God's Window, which is pictured overleaf, for the breath-taking view and an idea of the terrain we're going to cover. From here, it's as if you can see to the end of the earth! Mpumalanga's most famous attraction is the Kruger National Park, about a thousand metres below the look-out from God's Window. This is also an excellent spot to peer into the dizzying Motlatse River Canyon, an iconic image often used in South African tourist brochures.

The canyon is the third largest in the world and *the* largest green canyon, with its lush subtropical vegetation. You can't drive into the canyon, but the adventurous can try their hand at hiking or river rafting. If, like me, you're not the greatest athlete in the world, you can travel along the canyon's rim at a snail's pace and drink in its splendour.

The patient hands of time have helped shape Mpumalanga. And if you're still standing after the amazing view of the Motlatse River Canyon, make sure you have enough air to take in the utterly incredible site of Bourke's Luck Potholes, pictured overleaf, where the gentle strength of nature has carved shapes beyond your imagination.

Down in the subtropical Lowveld all manner of crops, including fruit, nuts, tea and coffee, grow with supernatural vigour. With its hot summers and mild winters the area is ideal for the production of bananas, mangoes, granadillas and avocado pears.

Ulusaba, Sir Richard Branson's private game reserve deep in Big Five territory, is the perfect place to think, to listen and to reflect. On the terrace at night you feel you can just about touch the stars. It is just a stone's throw from South Africa's iconic Kruger National Park where some of the world's top predators roam the plains and where some 150 species of mammals and 500 bird species make their home. The best thing to do is to switch off your city signals and tune in to animal behaviour.

This is my first visit to the Kruger Park. In the late nineteenth century, gold prospectors and big game hunters flocked to this region. Conservationists prevailed on the then-President of the South African Republic, Paul Kruger, to protect the area. Although credited with having the vision to create a wildlife haven, Kruger was apparently a keen hunter and, according to the first warden, James Stevenson-Hamilton, Kruger 'never in his life thought of animals except as biltong'. The Park's main camp is Skukuza – the site of two museums and a library that chronicle the Park's history and development.

The Kruger National Park has a complex social history. When the Park was declared, people who had been living on the land were forcibly removed. After apartheid was introduced in the mid-twentieth century, the Park's location along the border of Mozambique assumed increasingly strategic significance. By the 1970s and 80s many of the game rangers in the Park had worked for the South African Defence Force. They were equipped to manage the wildlife, and human refugees and/or freedom fighters too. In 1985, an estimated 49 tonnes of ivory left the country illegally, although it is unclear who did the poaching.

In 1998 former President Nelson Mandela visited the Park, not to hunt, but for a massive eightieth birthday party, attended by thousands of children. The following day he married Graça Machel, widow of Samora Machel, the first democratically elected president of Mozambique.

As a country, we have closed the book on many a dark chapter. There is much to celebrate, such as the inspirational Mbombela Stadium in Nelspruit, capital city of Mpumalanga. It was the only 2010 Soccer World Cup stadium designed by South Africans! With its zebra skin seats, giraffe-like roof supports and Ndebele colours, the structure is uniquely Mpumalangan.

Wherever you go in Mpumalanga the region's artistry bubbles to the surface – from the ubiquitous wood carvers to batik and sandstone specialists, and from candle-makers to iron mongers.

One of South Africa's greatest ever artists, Gerard Sekoto, is from this region. Sekoto was born at the German Lutheran Botshabelo Mission in Middelburg. After moving to Johannesburg, he eventually went into exile in France in 1947. Sekoto never came home, but his memories of life in South Africa live on in galleries and private collections across the world.

LIMPOPO

Land of Myths and Legends

Limpopo is a land of myths and legends, of prehistoric forests where the ancestors whisper through the leaves of upside-down trees and ancient history bursts from mineral-rich soil to shatter the illusions of the modern world. It is South Africa's gateway to the rest of Africa, sharing borders with Zimbabwe, Botswana and Mozambique.

Where South Africa, Zimbabwe and Botswana meet, and at the confluence of the Shashi and Limpopo Rivers, is the ancient site of Mapungubwe – which means 'the place where jackals eat' in the Venda language.

More than a thousand years ago Mapungubwe was the centre of the largest kingdom in Southern Africa and through its trade in gold and ivory with China, India and Egypt, it was the gateway to the world. The significance of Mapungubwe as a cultural landscape is evident in the interaction between humans and nature. The people made use of the environment for specific reasons like, for instance, the Limpopo River. Access to the river connected them with areas along the Indian Ocean coastline and meant that Mapungubwe became an important trading centre between 900 and 1300.

It is believed that the gold might have come from ancient gold mines in Zimbabwe because there are no gold mines, nor any trace of the metal, around Mapungubwe. When the people of Mapungubwe left in 1300, possibly as a result of severe climate change, they moved to Great Zimbabwe, which was the civilisation that began just after 1300. The pottery artefacts from Great Zimbabwe show a mixture of Shona, Venda and Sotho influence.

Ironically, part of what makes us call the Mapungubwe society 'sophisticated' is that with these riches came class distinction and the inequitable distribution of wealth. The ruling class lived on the top of the hill, while the commoners lived below and served them.

Mapungubwe National Park is a transfrontier park and World Heritage Site in one. It is a land full of secrets and mysteries, not least the Secret Lake, Fundudzi, that lies hidden in a valley below the Soutpansberg. It is the legendary home of ancestral spirits and the Venda python god of fertility. 'Fundudzi' means 'to bend', as in bending down and viewing the river through your legs to greet the spirits. This traditional salute is called the *ukodola*.

Also rooted in the mysteries of forgotten worlds are the ruins of the royal citadel at Thulamela. Close to the Zimbabwe and Mozambique borders in the very north of the Kruger National Park in an area called Pafuri, these ruins date back to between the fifteenth and seventeenth centuries and provide clues to another sophisticated society that had trade links with the Far East as well as West Africa.

Pafuri is today called the Makuleke Contractual Park. The story of the Makuleke people is a truly exquisite South African story of the triumph of right over wrong. Centuries ago, the Makuleke occupied this land between the Limpopo and Luvuvhu Rivers. They set down deep roots in this soil. The graves of generations of ancestors are here. But in 1969 the people were removed to make way for the expansion of the Kruger Park.

The word 'removed' does not tell half of this harrowing story. The people were forced, at gunpoint, to set fire to their own dwellings and were loaded on to trucks and dumped 70 kilometres outside the Park. Sometimes we forget too easily that what happened to tribal people here is totally unacceptable. The Chief told me that people were actually given matchboxes and told to go and set their homes alight or be shot.

In 1998, the Kruger Park's centenary year, the Makuleke community celebrated the return of their land. It was the first time in South African history that an indigenous community succeeded in winning the restitution of their land rights to national park land. It was agreed that the community would co-manage the land with the Park, and derive revenue from tourist lodges. A win-win situation was achieved: the conservation area remains intact and the people's rights and dignity are restored.

Despite the fact that the Makuleke people endured so much suffering they have no hatred in their hearts: we thank them that they have not been filled with anger, and hope the things that they long for, to fully develop their land as a heritage site, will remind the world of some of the bad things that happened here and how people can overcome their ignorance.

The Makuleke Tribal Council used to meet in the shade of this giant baobab. It is said that this is a special kind of tree. Legend has it that the baobabs were uprooted and turned upside down by angry gods. So, it looks as though their roots are reaching into the sky – perhaps begging for forgiveness . . .

Some say baobabs are enchanted because they can live for up to a thousand years, their roots stretching for kilometres under the earth. Their resilience and stature suggest that they could hold the memories of Africa.

Their distinct ecosystem supports both plants and animals: birds, bats and insects call these trees home, while elephants, antelopes and baboons feed on their fruit and strip their bark. They have been used by African people for centuries as houses, prisons, pubs, storage barns, and even as bus stops. The baobab really is a one-stop shop in the bush!

Another marvel of nature in this land of plenty is the rare and ancient cycad, a plant often referred to as a 'living fossil'. Cycads have been strictly protected by the Modjadji Rain Queen for generations. The first of these matriarchs is said to have fled here from Zimbabwe in the sixteenth century, bringing the rainmaking secrets of her family with her. Modjadji means 'queen mother' and she commands respect far and wide – even the fearless Shaka once sent emissaries to seek her counsel. Thus have she and the cycads lived in relative seclusion and protection throughout the centuries.

If you are still not convinced that Limpopo's trees are special, you probably haven't heard of the marula, which grows up to 18 metres high. Legend has it that elephants eat the fruit of this tree and become tipsy, but the scientists are sceptical. The marula has separate male and female trees with the female tree producing up to 500 kilograms of marula fruit in a season. The Venda people believe that if a pregnant woman drinks an infusion of tea made from the bark of the male tree, she'll bear a son, while an infusion from the bark of the female tree delivers a daughter. If a child of the opposite sex is born, it's said to be very special, having defied the spirits.

Wood sculpting is traditionally a male occupation among the Venda people, while ceramic work is reserved for women. In the mid-1970s Noria Mabasa challenged this convention when she began to sculpt in wood. This amazing, self-taught artist has found her place in the world and her name, reputation and work have travelled far and wide.

Another internationally acclaimed wood sculptor was Jackson Hlungwani, who passed away in 2010. Hlungwani had no formal training, but in the late-1970s he had a mystical experience that elevated his work from the skilful to the extraordinary. His most famous work, 'New Jerusalem', was originally housed at his home but it was dismantled in the 1980s when he won fame and pieces were sent to galleries around the world.

Limpopo is a place of dense bush and ancient secrets. It is a place of inspiration and reconciliation, a touchstone of our past and an ode to our resilience and our future.

GAUTENG

A Tale of Three Cities

South Africa's smallest province is also its richest, most populous and most powerful. With the economic hub of Johannesburg, the country's most populous urban black township, Soweto, and Pretoria, the seat of government in the north, Gauteng's golden finger is truly on South Africa's pulse.

It was in Gauteng where South Africa's political leaders, Nelson Mandela and F W de Klerk among them, negotiated our miraculous peaceful settlement. It was in Gauteng that Madiba was sworn in as the first president of all the people. And it was here that South Africa lifted the Rugby World Cup in 1995, and the African Cup of Nations football trophy the following year.

But long, long before the birth of Madiba, about a thousand years ago, the land was occupied first by San and Khoikhoi people, and later by early Bantu people whose languages originated in the Niger-Congo region of central Africa. The arrival of white people on ox wagons from the south was to alter the landscape forever.

By the 1830s Afrikaners, displeased with the relatively liberal treatment of slaves and servants by the ruling English in the Cape, embarked on what is historically known as the Great Trek into the northern and eastern regions of the land. It was a journey of adventure, discovery and land acquisition.

The Great Trek led to the creation of several Boer republics, of which the Transvaal, with its capital at Pretoria, was one. The discovery of gold in 1886 transformed a muddy camp in the old Transvaal into a bustling tent town of tens of thousands of people, and then into the city paved with gold that we know today as Johannesburg. Soweto, an acronym for South Western Townships, is the giant dormitory suburb for black labour spawned by Johannesburg.

It is not clear who discovered the main gold reef in Johannesburg, but it was probably a man called George. George Walker, George Harrison and George Honeyball were all frontiersman, drifters in search of a mining fortune. Walker and Harrison (the latter previously a gold digger in Australia) met on the Free State coal mines. Honeyball was the nephew of the owner of Langlaagte farm where the discovery of gold was first made. All three Georges laid claim to the discovery and historians have been unable to separate their contentions. But regardless of who picked up that first golden rock, it triggered an international stampede of people from all over the world, intent on seeking their fortunes.

The best place to learn about the gold rush that set the pace for years to come in the City of Gold, Egoli, or Jozi, as we like to call it today, is Gold Reef City. This historical theme park to the south of the city offers a wide variety of entertainments echoing the buzz of today's city.

Another South African landmark that was built about a hundred years ago is the Union Buildings. This traditional seat of South African power is strategically situated on top of Meintjieskop, the highest point in Pretoria. The Union Buildings were designed by Herbert Baker, an English architect who left an indelible and majestic mark on the South African landscape. When the Boer Republics of the Transvaal and Orange Free State united with the Cape and Natal Colonies in 1910 to establish the Union of South Africa the Union Buildings were built to house the government.

These buildings have seen their share of excitement. In 1956, 20 000 women converged here to protest against the racist laws of the day. In 1994, it was the ceremonial setting for the beginning of the new South Africa with the inauguration of Nelson Mandela as the first president of the 'new' South Africa. Since 1994, when South Africans voted overwhelmingly for non-racial governance, the Union Buildings have witnessed the once inconceivable notion of black and white legislators working together.

Newtown is today the heart of Johannesburg's inner city regeneration and reinvention. The Newtown Cultural Precinct houses three theatres, two art galleries and a Saturday morning flea market. The Market Theatre, known internationally as South Africa's 'Theatre of Struggle' was founded in 1976 by stage directors Mannie Manim and the late Barney Simon. The cultural precinct is steeped in South African history, and places to visit include the Sci-Bono Discovery Centre, Museum Africa, the Oriental Plaza, and the restored Kippies.

Right next door to the Market Theatre you will find Kippies, originally a jazz venue named after legendary South African saxophonist and musical genius, Kippie Moeketsi. Kippies, today a jazz museum, was the place to hear great music in the 1980s and 90s. Kippie Moeketsi was one of the members of the influential Jazz Epistles – a 1950s bepop band, whose other members included Dollar Brand, Hugh Masekela, Jonas Gwangwa and Johnny Gertse.

It is possible today to visit the former home of Nelson Mandela at 8115 Vilakazi Street in Orlando West, Soweto. This was the first home Mandela owned and lived in with his first wife, Evelyn Mase, and his second wife, Winnie Madikizela. Vilakazi Street is known as the only road in the world to have been home to two winners of the Nobel Peace Prize, namely Nelson Mandela and Desmond Tutu. I can assure you we did not plan it that way.

Soweto will always be remembered for sparking the youth insurrection on 16 June 1976 in protest against a third-rate education system and being forced to learn in Afrikaans. On that day, led by Teboho 'Tsietsi' Mashinini, thousands of schoolchildren took to the streets, and their courage reverberated across the land. Of course, the police responded brutally. Among the first children to die was Hector Pieterson. Today, 16 June is commemorated as Youth Day in South Africa.

On a township tour to Soweto visitors are able to step into South Africa's troubled past at the Hector Pieterson Museum, the Tsietsi Mashinini Memorial, the Freedom Charter Monument in Kliptown, and the Walter Sisulu Square of Dedication – with the contemporary bustle of Soweto all around them.

Another important monument to the twentieth century struggles of South Africans is the Apartheid Museum. Located on the doorstep of Gold Reef City, this museum will take you through recent South African history, the rise and fall of apartheid, within a space designed to underscore the oppressive atmosphere of the story.

The hopes and dreams of the entire country focused on Soccer City in Soweto in the winter of 2010. Soccer City, famously the first African venue to host an opening match of a FIFA World Cup soccer match, was also the first place in Johannesburg where the freed Nelson Mandela delivered a speech.

Gauteng may be the smallest province in South Africa, but it has a heart of gold that beats at a frenetic pace. It is South Africa's engine room and most cosmopolitan destination, a land of opportunity, acceptance and triumph. Once the bug bites, like many of those who now call it home, you may never want to leave!

NORTHERN CAPE

Diamond Province

The Northern Cape is our largest province, encompassing almost a third of South Africa. Like the rest of South Africa, this land is full of surprises. Vast, sometimes harsh, yet bursting with life and hope, you will find that what may at first appear barren is, when you look carefully, more beautiful than you could imagine.

Here we find the breathtaking Augrabies Falls, called Ankoerebis or 'place of big noises' by the original Khoikhoi residents of the area. Three times more water pours over these falls than the Niagara Falls on the border of the United States and Canada. It's the water of the Orange River – the longest river in South Africa, stretching all the way from the Drakensberg Mountains to the Atlantic Ocean. The Orange River is a spectacular introduction to the natural wealth of this area: it is the lifeblood of South Africa, providing water for irrigation, and hydroelectric energy from the Gariep and Vanderkloof dams.

The Northern Province is also the starting point of a journey that had a powerful, wonderful, and terrible influence on the history of South Africa. In 1869, a boy called Erasmus Jacobs found a stone on his father's farm on the Orange River. His mother mentioned how shiny the stone was to a neighbour, who offered to buy the stone, but she gave it to him for free. That stone was the Eureka Diamond, the first diamond found in South Africa, and its discovery would trigger an incredible scramble by people from all over the world wanting to lay their hands on South Africa's wealth.

     The South African Story with Archbishop Desmond Tutu

How much of a scramble? Just look at this hole!

This particular piece of land was once a hill on a farm owned by two brothers, Diederik Arnoldus and Johannes Nicholas De Beer. They found diamonds on their farm, and people flooded in to dig them out. This hole was dug by hand. Some people say this is the biggest man-made hole in the world but, actually, that's not strictly true – that hole is in Jagersfontein, south-east of here. But this is the *deepest* hole dug by hand, originally going down to a depth of 240 metres.

People came from all over Europe and Africa to look for diamonds and of course, black people were welcome as a source of cheap labour.

The British, who had control of much of South Africa at the time, were quick to annex the area. The Boers felt it should form part of 'their' Orange Free State Republic because it lay between the Orange and Vaal rivers; but ultimately the town at the centre of the rush was named after the British Secretary of State for the Colonies at the time, John Wodehouse, First Earl of Kimberley.

In the beginning, Kimberley was a shanty town. But because it was considered the land of opportunity it became the fastest-growing city in Africa, the first town in the southern hemisphere to install electric street lighting – and the Kimberley Gentlemen's Club claimed more millionaires per square foot than anywhere else on earth.

Among the colonial prospectors drawn to Kimberley were an ex-prizefighter, Barney Barnato, and an 18-year-old boy called Cecil John Rhodes. A Jewish Cockney, Barnato grew up in London. He arrived at Kimberley with nothing of value but a box of cigars, which he sold to the miners. He used the money to start buying diamonds, and then pieces of land, called claims.

Cecil John Rhodes was doing the same thing, and the two men raced to control all of the mines. In 1888, Rhodes bought up all of Barney Barnato's claims for five million pounds, which at the time was the largest cheque ever written.

Rhodes's De Beers company, named after the brothers who originally owned the farm, went on to control 90 per cent of the world's diamond production.

Rhodes had his own personal railway carriage and was the ultimate colonial. He believed the resources of Africa were there for the taking. He once said, 'I would annex the planets if I could; I often think of that. It makes me sad to see them so clear and yet so far.'

Steam locomotives were part of his big plan to connect the Cape to Cairo by railway, and take all the territory along the way into the British Empire. Rhodes was granted a charter by the British government to police, rule, and make treaties to take over Africa from the Limpopo up to the great lakes of Central Africa. He used his powers to take over the territories called Northern and Southern Rhodesia, which later became Zambia and Zimbabwe. He was also a member of parliament in South Africa.

One of the people who made their home in Kimberley was a hero of our country: Sol Plaatje. A journalist, writer, translator, intellectual and politician, he was among the most gifted and versatile South Africans of his generation and was at the forefront of the public affairs of African people for the greater part of his adult life. He was a founding member of the South African Native National Congress, which would later become the African National Congress. He was a brilliant man, fluent in seven languages. Here in Kimberley he was the editor and part owner of two newspapers.

In days gone by, the first people – the Khoi and the San – occupied vast territories across South Africa. But after being decimated by sickness, hunted down like vermin and assimilated into other ethnic groups, the last of these people today occupy the wide open, arid spaces of the Richtersveld and the Kalahari. These are places of wonder, of surreal moon landscapes, stark white gravel plains and red sand dunes.

In 1999, the so-called Bushmen of the Kalahari received vast landholdings in the area from the government as restitution for their suffering and dispossession, including a share of the Kgalagadi Transfrontier Park, where cheetah dice with springbok in a deadly race for survival.

Not all land restitution stories have happy endings. In the Kalahari, the Bushmen are now significant landowners, but they are so poor, and have been downtrodden and marginalised for so many years, that many are functionally unable to build better lives for themselves.

The South African Story with Archbishop Desmond Tutu

Towards the end of apartheid, when some form of democratic settlement began to seem inevitable, there was talk in the Afrikaner community of creating their own homeland in South Africa. Grand visions of carving up the country eventually came down to the town of Orania which was purchased lock, stock and barrel by members of the Volk.

About 600 Afrikaners trekked here in 1991, modelling their separate and largely self-sufficient community to some extent on the Israeli kibbutz system. Among them were academics, engineers, farmers and teachers – and the widow and family of the former South African prime minister H F Verwoerd, known as the father of apartheid. Their purpose was to maintain Afrikaner culture. They have quietly got on with their lives in this corner of Africa that has become distinguishable for its lack of pigmented people.

One of the most extraordinary moments of reconciliation in post-apartheid South Africa was Nelson Mandela's visit to Orania in 1995 to meet Betsie Verwoerd, the frail widow of H F Verwoerd.

It's surprising moments like these, of people reaching out across divides, of hope from unexpected quarters, of flowers blooming in the desert – of the complexity of the fabric that weaves us together – that define our beautiful land.

EASTERN CAPE

Liberation Route

From this rugged land, where waterfalls plunge down sheer rock faces directly into a churning sea, rose many of the giants of the South African liberation movement: Steve Biko, Robert Sobukwe, Oliver Tambo, Nelson Mandela.

The Eastern Cape is a place of incongruities, where apartheid neglect allowed the natural splendour – and the people's spirit of resistance – to flourish unhindered. There is no gold here, no platinum or diamonds. The Eastern Cape's wealth is embedded in the visual richness of its landscapes, its cultural traditions, its human warmth.

Our journey to the Eastern Cape starts in Qunu, where Nelson Mandela grew up after his father was deposed as chief at nearby Mvezo by a white magistrate, for alleged insubordination. And it was to Qunu that Mandela returned after his release from prison to build a retirement home.

Today, a hilltop above his home in Qunu is one of the sites of the Nelson Mandela Museum which first opened in the regional capital Mthatha on the tenth anniversary of Mandela's freedom. Visitors to the museum gain unique insights into the places and culture and thinking that created the Father of our Nation.

Local youth gather here, at the museum's Youth and Heritage Centre in Qunu, to retrace Mandela's footsteps, to learn about his values and principles so that they will be able to preserve his legacy for years to come. In Mthatha, the museum houses gifts that President Mandela accepted on behalf of all South Africans from admirers across the world.

The Nelson Mandela Museum sites are located in what was known as the Transkei homeland under the apartheid government. Homelands, also known as Bantustans, were in fact nominally independent banana republics with puppet governments answerable to Pretoria. By confining the majority of black South Africans to their own 'independent' countries, the theory went, whites could continue to control the most valuable land and economic resources.

The former capital city of the Ciskei homeland, Bhisho, is today the capital city of the Eastern Cape.

After we voted apartheid into history in 1994, South Africa established a Truth and Reconciliation Commission to help heal our wounds. The commission created a platform for ordinary South Africans to recount the stories of their past, and for perpetrators of violence – of all political persuasions – to make full disclosures of their activities in exchange for amnesty.

It was a gruelling, grim, yet glorious process that began here, in the East London City Hall in 1996, with the searing testimonies of the widows of the so-called Cradock Four, Matthew Goniwe, Sparrow Mkhonto, Fort Calata and Sicelo Mhlauli, murdered by security policemen ten years before.

During that first week of hearings a statue of slain Black Consciousness icon Steve Biko was erected outside the City Hall. When we arrived for work the following morning the statue had been defaced.

The stories of victims and perpetrators held South Africans and the rest of the world spellbound. The Truth and Reconciliation Commission helped lay the foundations for forgiveness and common understanding from which all South Africans could move forward.

East London is also home to some fascinating natural history. The only dodo egg in existence is on display at the East London Museum in its natural history gallery, as well as an impressive exhibit of the rare coelacanth fish. The coelacanth was thought to be extinct until it was spotted on a fishing boat in the East London harbour in 1938. One of its most striking features – its leg-like fins – has prompted many scientists to believe that the coelacanth represents an early step in the evolution of fish to terrestrial four-legged animals like amphibians.

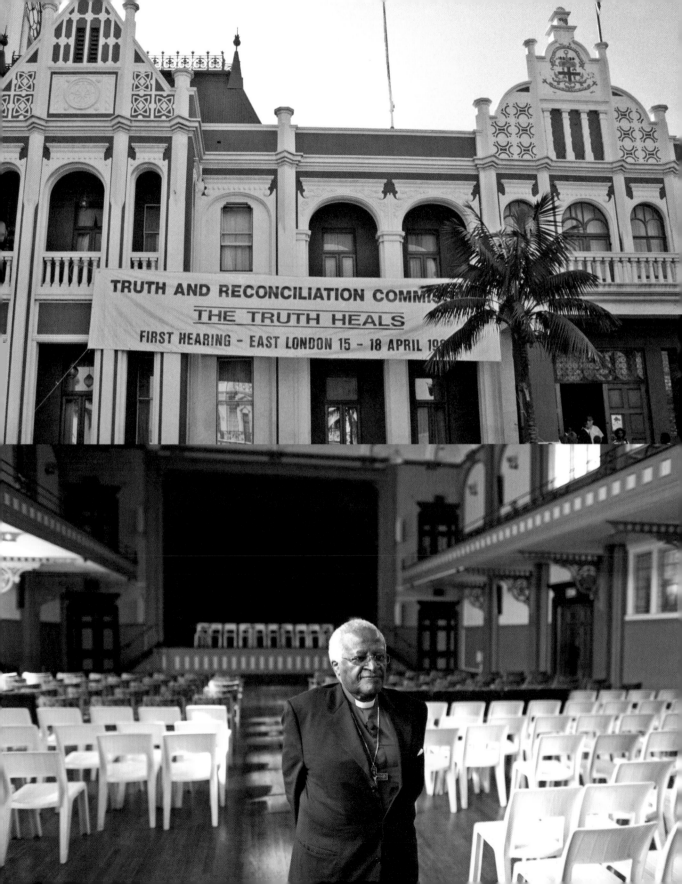

Port Elizabeth is the biggest city in the Eastern Cape. It has many nicknames, including the abbreviation PE, the Xhosa eBhayi, which means 'the bay', and the 'Friendly City'. Port Elizabeth is home to the Nelson Mandela Stadium. In order to counter strong prevailing winds, the stadium's roof was designed more or less in the shape of a sunflower.

Travelling inland from the Friendly City offers up some interesting gems. Graaff-Reinet, the fourth oldest town in the country, has more than two hundred buildings that have been declared national monuments. This was the birthplace of Robert Sobukwe, the founder of the Pan Africanist Congress, a great thinking South African whose contribution is too often ignored.

In winter, writers, artists, performers and musicians descend on Grahamstown for the annual National Arts Festival which has hosted some groundbreaking productions. Grahamstown was founded by English settlers after their en masse arrival at Algoa Bay (now Port Elizabeth) in 1820. The Settlers Monument commemorates their coming and their contribution to South African society. Appropriately, Grahamstown is also home to the oldest newspaper in South Africa, *Grocott's Mail*, and one of the country's oldest universities – Rhodes University.

The Eastern Cape is renowned for its educational institutions. A little town called Alice, inland from East London, is home to two famous places of learning: Lovedale, a mission school for high school boys, and Fort Hare University, which offered a Western-style education to young black students.

Steve Biko attended Lovedale for a short while, and Thabo Mbeki, South Africa's second democratically elected president, was famously expelled from Lovedale in his final year for the role he played in organising a class boycott in 1959.

Fort Hare is just across the Tyume River from Lovedale and is the alma mater of Nelson Mandela, Govan Mbeki, Oliver Tambo and Robert Sobukwe. The extreme climate in Alice inspired many a deep thinker and fanned the flames of resistance!

Extreme weather on the Eastern Cape's Wild Coast has been responsible for its fair share of drama. From the late 1400s, a few centuries before GPS was invented, sailors frequently miscalculated their bearings and ran aground. The Portuguese *Nossa Senhora de Belem*, ran into trouble south of the Umzimvubu River, the *Dodington* was stranded at Algoa Bay and the *Grosvenor* was bashed to pieces off the Pondoland coast.

Port St Johns at the mouth of the Umzimvubu River is another feast for the eyes and soul. Many believe that the Wild Coast is the jewel of South Africa where one can walk along the poetic coastline with the Indian Ocean roaring sweet nothings on the one hand and the Transkei Hills whispering their secrets on the other.

A little further north the Mkhambathi nature reserve, where waterfalls cascade directly into the sea, is one of a number of reserves that have been established in recent times to ensure the preservation of this untamed coast.

And just when you thought you'd seen it all in the Eastern Cape, this extraordinary land offers one last treasure: a high altitude ski resort on the slopes of the Southern Drakensberg. Yes, it snows in Africa, and it most certainly snows on the Drakensberg.

With its traditional villages and modern towns, the Eastern Cape straddles the old and the new, a living lesson in how the past has influenced the present. With its tempestuous seas, extreme climates, pristine beaches, and snow, this is truly a world in one province!

KWAZULU-NATAL

Kings and Leaders

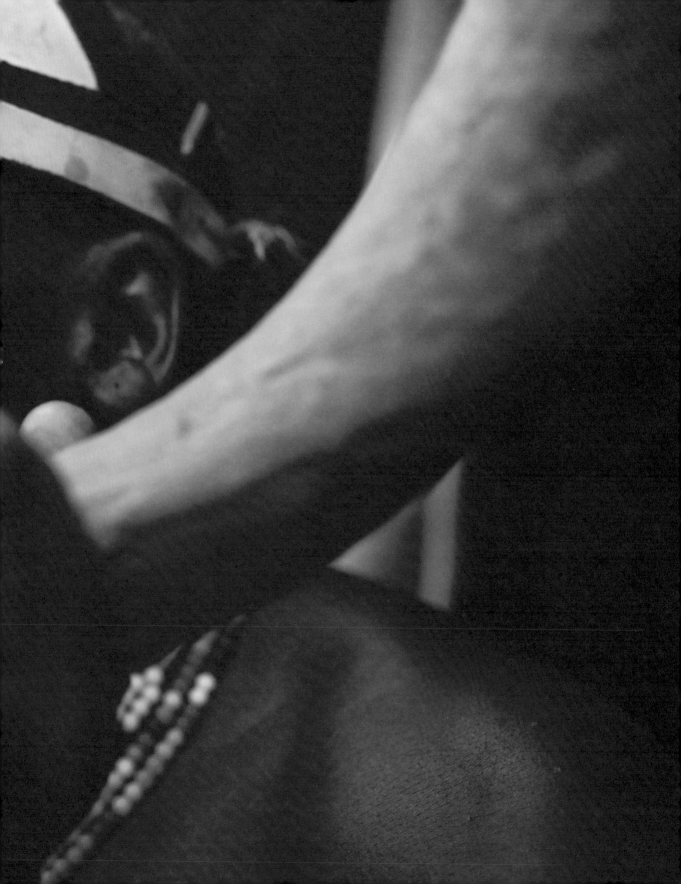

KwaZulu-Natal's story is surely one of the most fascinating to relate, an epic tale of warrior kings, cultural diversity and breathtaking World Heritage Sites. It is a story told through rock paintings, the rich oral history and traditions of the great Zulu nation, the arrival of European settlers and sugar plantations and, later, indentured workers from India.

It was these verdant hills that warrior King Shaka bestrode, this great port city of Durban that Mahatma Gandhi called home – and along a rural railroad track that Africa's first Nobel Peace Laureate, banished by apartheid decree, died mysteriously.

Our story begins in the KwaZulu-Natal interior, where a mountain range of exquisite beauty cuts a swathe across the land. These mountains are known as uKhahlamba (the Barrier of Spears), or Drakensberg (Dragon Mountain). Their slopes were originally the domain of the San – the first people – who left tens of thousands of rock paintings telling the story of their lives. Scientists have established, by carbon dating rock art, that San people were living here 100 000 years ago, when the great migration of pastoralists from central Africa began thousands of kilometres to the north.

Needing fertile grazing for their cattle, but finding themselves hemmed in between the Sahara Desert and tropical rain forests, these pastoralists migrated east across the Rift Valley and the Lake Belt, then south through what is now Mozambique, to KwaZulu-Natal. They brought with them South Africa's first cattle. It is said that the click sounds in the Nguni languages were assimilated through their interaction with the San people.

Down at the coast, several centuries later, KwaZulu-Natal was fast becoming a fashionable destination for overseas visitors. When Portuguese explorer Vasco da Gama set eyes on these shores on 25 December 1497, he named the land 'Natal', Portuguese for 'Christmas'.

In the nineteenth century, competition for land grew intense. King Shaka – the 'Black Napoleon' – organised his people into a military machine that forged the Zulu nation. Other clans and chiefdoms were protected in exchange for providing army recruits, women and cattle. Those who did not comply were forcibly assimilated. By 1819 the Zulu nation was the mightiest in Southern Africa.

It was King Shaka who agreed to the establishment of a British settlement at Port Natal. A party of twenty-five men had arrived from the Cape and established a settlement on the northern shore of the Bay of Natal. During a meeting of residents in 1835 it was decided to build a capital town, to be named after Sir Benjamin d'Urban, then governor of the Cape Colony.

In years to come relations between Zulus and colonists deteriorated markedly. The might of the Zulu army clashed with Voortrekkers of Dutch origin who had arrived overland from the Cape to briefly establish an independent republic with its own capital, Pietermaritzburg.

Years later, at the battle of Isandlwana in 1879, King Cetshwayo inflicted the heaviest defeat the British had ever suffered in the colonies. More than 1 300 British soldiers died on a single day. The British overturned this defeat six months later, burning King Cetshwayo's royal homestead to the ground following the battle of Ulundi.

KwaZulu-Natal is indeed littered with sites of war. Its Battlefields Route – commemorating wars between colonial powers, and between colonial powers and local people – is a popular destination for scholars, historians and tourists.

At Phezulu Cultural Village, the Gasa clan is occupied in the altogether more peaceful pursuit of affording visitors insights into the rich fabric of Zulu culture. It is an opportunity to savour the taste and feel the rhythm of Africa – and an unforgettable experience!

The short-lived Voortrekker capital of Pietermaritzburg is now the capital city of KwaZulu-Natal, seat of the democratically elected provincial parliament, where gentlemen still dine at the Victoria Club under the stern gaze of Queen Victoria herself. The Pietermaritzburg City Hall is one of the finest examples of Victorian architecture in South Africa.

It was the British who introduced sugar cane to KwaZulu-Natal. India's rural population had seen opportunities for land tenure diminish, and the prospect of a new life in the Natal Colony was not unappealing. In 1860 two ships pioneered the introduction of indentured labourers to our shores: the *Belvedere* from Calcutta, and the *Truro* from Madras. Three hundred and eighty-four vessels would ply this route over the next fifty years, bearing 150 000 precious souls.

The social and working conditions the newcomers found on their arrival were far from rosy. Complaints about the treatment of Indians by colonial employers ranged from flogging and assaults to irregular payment and rations, unwarranted salary deductions, extra working hours, poor medical facilities and non-payment of termination monies to those seeking repatriation.

This was the Port Natal-Durban that a young London-trained barrister discovered when he stepped ashore in 1893. His name was Mohandas Karamchand Gandhi, and he had been contracted for a year to pursue a 40 000 pound civil claim on behalf of Dada Abdullah and Company against two rival merchants.

The case for which he'd come to South Africa was on the court roll in Pretoria, and this was Gandhi's destination when he boarded a train in Durban in June 1893. Dumped on to the platform, in Pietermaritzburg, for refusing to give up a 'Whites Only' compartment, he spent the night meditating in a draughty waiting room. He said later it was here that his commitment to active non-violence, or passive resistance, began. People who thought they had humiliated him did not know that they had started a movement for freedom.

The continuing ill-treatment of Indian indentured workers, together with the disenfranchisement of immigrant Indians, commanded Gandhi's attention, and he was to remain in South Africa for considerably longer than anticipated. The Durban Indian Committee had already initiated the first South African Indian political campaign, petitioning no less a figure than Queen Victoria herself. Gandhi suggested the formation of a permanent political structure to be called the Natal Indian Congress and the organisation was founded in August 1894.

In 1913, indentured Indian labourers went on strike – initially in the coal mining area of Newcastle in northern Natal, followed by Durban and adjacent coastal belts. These were the first ever strikes in the country's history. Gandhi was arrested thrice in November 1913, and sentenced to a total of twelve months' imprisonment.

Mahatma Gandhi may have been of Indian origin, but he was a South African pathfinder, a leader and a teacher. With his passive resistance, he set an example that many of us tried to emulate over the next hundred years of our struggle for equal rights, non-violent change, tolerance and love.

A young teacher raised in Groutville, north of Durban, would have applauded Gandhi's actions. A man of powerful logic and a keen sense of justice, uncompromising in his stance against racialism, tribalism and exclusivity, the teacher gave up his career when called by elders of his clan to come home and lead. Forced by the government to choose between chieftainship and politics, he chose politics. He was deposed as chief in 1952, and elected president-general of the African National Congress the same year. Harassed by apartheid authorities, jailed, tried for treason and banned, Chief Albert John Luthuli was confined to the Lower Tugela region of KwaZulu-Natal from 1952 until his death in mysterious circumstances in 1967 – he was knocked down by a train. Today, visitors to the area can visit the Luthuli Museum and view the plaque next to the railway tracks where the great man died.

South Africa's story is one of many threads woven together over time into a vibrant tapestry of hope. We live in nine distinctively different provinces and have eleven official languages. We are learning to speak with one voice.

We come from a turbulent past. We really were a very unattractive caterpillar that has become a butterfly of exquisite beauty. We have unfurled our wings and taken flight, together. We have glimpsed tomorrow.

The sky is our only limit.

ACKNOWLEDGEMENTS

These are some of the people without whom *The South African Story with Archbishop Desmond Tutu* would not have been told...

Archbishop Desmond and Mrs Leah Tutu

Scott and Christy Wallace, executive producers of *The South African Story with Archbishop Desmond Tutu*

Members of the Tutu support staff
Mthunzi Gxashe
Vivian Ford

Co-writers and researchers
Lauren Beukes
Tina-Louise Smith
Sam Wilson
Helen Atty
Twanji Kalula
Priya Reddy
Glenda Nevill

The Clockwork Zoo production team
Glenn Gillis and Sean Rogers
Jemima Spring
Liezel Vermeulen

Editors of the television series
Ronet van der Walt
Katherine Millar
Matthys Pretorius

The Oryx Multimedia Productions team
Nita Nagar and Alberic Vollmer – Graphic Design
Lindixolo Bhavuma – Logistics
Harlaine Wasser – Media Manager

All photography www.ORYX MEDIA.CO.ZA except:
Lion: *Florian Thieme*, page 56
Bourke's Luck Potholes: *SAMA Tours*, page 60
Gold Reef City Theme Park and Miner: *Gold Reef City Theme Park*, page 91
Port Elizabeth beach: *Ilonde van Hoolwerff / Art Publishers*, pages 126 and 127